Fourth Person Singular

Fourth Person Singular

Nuar Alsadir

First published 2017 by
Liverpool University Press
4 Cambridge Street
Liverpool
L69 7ZU

British Library Cataloguing-in-Publication data
A British Library CIP record is available

ISBN 978-1-78694-019-3 softback

Typeset by Carnegie Book Production, Lancaster
Printed and bound in Poland by Booksfactory.co.uk

From a certain point on, there is no more turning back.
That is the point that must be reached.

— Franz Kafka

The door to my interior was propped open and a fly buzzed in.

To repossess my thoughts as a car gets repossessed if payment hasn't been made—but what kind of debt is owed, and to whom?

The photos on the wall of his house: dashing then death, like the moment before fainting, the voices on the car radio shifting from the rear to the front speakers, *subito fortissimo*, then—

d   ing
ash

syncope

I stood in the loudness of my thoughts like a cut-out superimposed onto the background scene.

Shots of sidebar and awe—

Transparence interests me, wrote Louise Bourgeois in a notebook. I want to be transparent. If people could see through me, they could not help loving me, forgive me.

Within: a chattering of girls who talk & talk, starling
murmuration of mathematical chaos across my sky—

Why do you talk so much? What is it that you have to
hide?

I pace back and forth like indecision in an old movie.

All of my attention is on a hangnail—I move it to feel
the pain—

Thinking off the page: a plane circling over its
destination, waiting for a signal to land.

I stand in grass that grows to dune shack roofs, keep
to myself—a way of retaining my idea in head, being
protective (defensive?), not wanting to adjust the idea to
world?

A white truck pulled past the window like a linear wipe,
shifting my thoughts to a grainy blankness—

Objects that are near remain out of grasp.

The sun is most beautiful just before it rises, like the
unspoken before it reaches the world—

HD: I know, I feel/ the meaning that words hide;/ they are anagrams, cryptograms/ little boxes, conditioned/ to hatch butterflies...

Crows signal in the void, materialize what was already known, but elsewhere—

I said I couldn't, and all subsequent text messages were clip clip chopped shrubs, nothing out of order.

I smell it the way I smelled you were hiding something yesterday or a child can smell infection.

Washing lettuce: how the wet leaves sag like the face of propriety when it smiles, no contraction of the *m. orbicularis oculi*, no movement in the lower eyelid—

Every group has its emperor.

Don't waste your energy and your time—which belong to God—throwing stones at the dogs that bark at you on the way. Ignore them. Norman Mailer marked this passage in his copy of works of Josemaría Escrivá on a bookshelf in his dining room.

I am so much light, like the day: cold, but double sun because of snow: sun from above & sun from below—

The small pocket, merely decorative, is sewn shut, no place for holding—some people are like that, sewn pockets, can't hold a thing.

I follow rules the way others follow superstitions or a child follows a crab in sand, without realizing I am walking sideways.

Man's flight from mystery towards what is readily available, onward from one current thing to the next, passing the mystery by—this is *erring*.

All of my oddities make it difficult to generalize.

What works intellectually doesn't always work in the gut and vice versa—the basis of discord and interesting music.

Chairs in the waiting room are misaligned so that one person's thoughts do not catch on another's. Silence is a ballast, absorbing the current to keep it from growing, but eventually, as with fluorescent lights, a buzz will break through (magnetostriction), which will only intensify the impulse to turn away. How delicate, this determination not to connect!

If only the surface of the painting would crack and release the wild syntax of gulls, low-tide stench, hankering of gnats, something *real*—

Hemingway would record every detail around an event—say, a bomb exploding—then take out the event and leave only its reverberations. I have been walking through reverberations with no sense of what the event was.

In the 1980s, Coke ran an advertising campaign that involved collecting bottle caps. Each cap had a word or a letter written inside, and if you collected all of the caps necessary to read, "Coke The Real Thing," you'd win a spectacular prize. The trick was to flood the market with a seemingly infinite number of bottle caps with the words—and letters to the words—*Coke*, *The* and *Thing*, but to limit access to the *Real*. Yet maybe it was more lesson than trick. In Jacques Lacan's triad of the Symbolic, the Imaginary and the Real, you also can't get at the Real. The psychic market is similarly flooded with the Imaginary and the Symbolic—it's not about Coke, the actual drink, but the transcendent experience you imagine in drinking it, as well as the message your drinking Coke will transmit to yourself and others about who you are—

Maybe it's impossible to get Real, and that's the million-dollar revelation.

Why did they care so much, all the king's horses and all the king's men? Was nothing else happening in the kingdom? Was Humpty Dumpty somehow important to the greater good? Or was it the impulse to put the pieces back together again, revert to an idyllic image of cohesion, avoid fragmentation at all cost?

Picasso's faces are Humpty & loss. Tonight, I will go out with the face of shatter, Cubist celebration, without hankering to cohere—

I want to be/at least as alive as the vulgar.

We must avoid letting our desires, which are general, override the intuition that is specific.

A text message in the night poked into my dreams like a magnetic rod and scrambled them, redistributing the metal shavings.

On my way to the meeting: neither emperor nor bride, I will observe the courtly spectacle from afar.

Went to a party at ▬▬▬—everyone seemed the same, strangers.

God will vomit out the lukewarm.

A yes so out-of-tune it sounds like a no & I can't tell what I'm listening to—

Yesterday I passed a flattened rat on 3rd Avenue in front of The Original Zesty's. It lay like a pressed flower, with kept color, The Original Red & Grey.

Most of what happens does so without me, like revelation, the ocean pulling back unexpectedly.

All the clocks in this place are off. Midnight is morning and I'm late to my thoughts, catch only a wave of skirt as a door closes behind—

It seems right that the lines and curves of dream thoughts should be thick, written with marker.

Picked up slides of my biopsies: beautiful pink swirls, elongated *S*'s—

Does my heart sit on fault lines?

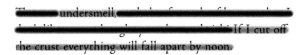

I'm tiptoeing around my life.

When I sand against the grain, the shape of the driftwood's surface is destroyed. Is it the same with thoughts, when you try to *have them* ~~as opposed to letting them tumble out as they already are?~~

What is beneath my feet—or beneath the beneath, the visible ground?

A murder of crows to the west—

I imagine some kind of end stop. A period, or a period followed by a page break, or just a page break with silence where the period would have been—

The dishes in my mind: the very knowledge of them, what needs to get done, keeps me from cooking something new.

They give me a bad feeling, like the smell of yeast—the thought of them smells like yeast.

Entirely taken up by the present, I could remember nothing.

Dinner at ▬▬▬ I was a hog, talking & talking. I surprise myself when I get that way, jabbing people's shins with my heels as I rush by—

Anxiety: regretting what I said. But it is not the *what* that makes me feel shame. Rather, it is the desire to be transparent, which is, transparently, the desire to be loved, forgiven, seen—

Prospect theory: we are wired to pay more attention to losses. Do you cut your losses in a bad situation or gamble to get back to zero or beyond? Most act aggressively in weakness, whereas Freud calls for mourning.

Despair, like central heat—

Thinking is interposed between feeling and action. Action evades thoughts & feelings.

Fear brings out the most counterintuitive behaviors, like leash aggression, barking at big dogs as a way of disowning your fear and projecting it into others.

Starling chatter flashing madly in the shade of the evergreen outside the Masonic Temple this first sunny morning, dogs pulling at their leashes, my throat, words flapping out of their drawers & unfolding chaotically as you approach—

Your silence: a tarp over the garden in winter— suffocating the weeds, yes, but what else besides?

Another storm: wind so strong it blew the door open three times in the night. Can there be revelation without chaos, recycling bins flying into the middle of the street?

You can't have an unconscious emotion. You may not know what thought an emotion is attached to, but you feel it.

██
███████████████████████████ and cars at night climbing in and out of dumpsters overflowing like the mind after war moving ██████████ so as not to recall ███████████ now broken and half sitting, half hanging from the sixth floor balcony like a memory—

The man across from me—lips narrowed, brows tilting downward towards his nose & falling into each other— stomps a foot. The stomp discharges his anger—a grain bounces off the door of the subway car and hits my eye—

A man possesses himself in flashes, and even when he possesses himself, he does not possess himself completely.

I have been lost [HTTP Error 404]—so why do I feel alive from the boot up?

I run the risk of fading. Yet, inside, such deep pink—

Anomaly: a white line on a black luggage belt that makes you recognize the movement in monotony.

Heidegger offers the example of a hammer seizing its actuality, revealing its form, only when broken. It is then that we no longer take the tool for granted. The hammer shifts from being ready-at-hand (to be used in the act of hammering) to present-at-hand (present, but without a use). An object needs to be defamiliarized in order to be grasped, understood as separate from its use (hammering). Like a mother, an object in use is phenomenologically transparent.

I am the center of every circle my dog circumferences, the spike implanted beneath the compass's hinge.

The only thing to hold on to is letting go.

Distance begins in betrayal

First learning to drive: busy highway, afraid to switch lanes and make exit possible

Is opportunity lost, or does it merely cycle out of view?

I only have a few minutes, so I'll have to go heavy on the triple back flips—not much time for filler, little dance steps to get to the corner of the mat.

In thinking of my answer to ▇ question, I used his name rather than the usual initial. Perhaps that abbreviation is a kind of conjugation—his initial exists in the present conditional, the present unreal, whereas

his name is in the past perfect. What do I ascribe to
him in the present? Or is language unnecessary when in
face of the *thing* sitting across from me, elbows on table,
leaning slightly forward?

The Other Person is always perceived as an other, but
in its concept it is the condition for all perception,
for others as for ourselves. It is the condition for our
passing from one world to another.

My desire displaced me from the moment, time became
oriented around what might come and, in order for
arrival, I willed its passing (a terrible thing).

Winter: overheated hallway, soup onions, the long
boil—

Maybe that is the danger of poetic thought, an escape
into a shadow world. But the *Real*—is it there, can
I approach it without going through something else,
wearing goggles or gloves?

My hand
is in the
mouth of   Mott between Broken and Spring.
the bark

So many seasons on the crosstown bus thinking of
you—

The cobbler shop: shoes stripped, hung from nails in the wall, soles open like thirsty dogs—

       my soul, too, opens like a thirsty dog—

It points me in a different direction, one I wasn't yet prepared to go in.

Thing theory: an object becomes a thing when it no longer works for us, when it breaks down and we can no longer simply *use* it. What was formerly a mere object becomes an object-to-subject relationship, lyric.

The crinkle of opening a gift: insect flying into glass or light.

That two-degrees-rotated-suspended-above-body-&-forward sensation, as though the anima were about to hit the ground face first & break a tooth at any second—

How anxiety leads to bad choices.

At the root of every triangle is a problematic attachment to a woman.

The things you don't want to see that ironically everyone shares with you—

At the dog park: weak dogs invite attack. The powerful ones have a nose for fear, like in middle school.

All shades of empty

The old man beside me, smell of soup, the unintended seeping out of us—

I feel the hum of the bus in the sole of my boot, electric ecstasy.

elecstasy

Autoplot: the unconscious's scheme to take over your story of self by creating an autopilot that overrides all other (conscious) renditions.

When you see a common practice disrupted, a delay in an everyday rhythm—being stuck in the subway tunnel between stations, silence inserting a pause in the volley-like exchange of conversation—the experience is stripped of its familiarity and, like Heidegger's broken hammer, yields its being, its *thingness*. The detainees at Abu Ghraib, in being given names according to the functions soldiers associated with them ("Taxi Cab Driver," "Rapist"), were ready-at-hand as opposed to present-at-hand, which perhaps contributed to the soldiers' objectification of them.

It's degrading to be reduced to concerns about survival—war brings people to that position.

*I don't sleep. My neighbor has a dog and whenever it starts
barking I run to the window. I don't want them to cut me
up like a chicken.*

All numbers in my mind—from my first phone number
to the addresses of former homes—fall into each
other like objects on a dresser shaken by a drawer
slammed shut or some other abruptness, quick closing,
unexpected departure.

What is your fear? Is it the moment when something
goes wrong and there is trouble or hurt, ball hit into
back, if boy?

He turned the page to a new chapter, this man on the
train who holds my interest, whose arm I read around
and over.

Girls in bright tank tops with moves that break dishes!

The oncoming train: its velocity throws onto me in a
sudden jolt of displaced area, as death must. But this
moment, still alive, horses in their sweaters grazing the
Scottish countryside, living after.

The fear of the fruit fly (I can smell it in its vile).

The normal is no longer available.

So much of the violence we encounter at the daily level is intrapsychic, between different parts of mind.

The lyric as a form of ego splitting, becoming multiple, monument to a state of knowing and not-knowing.

I have given a name to my shame and call it 'dog.'

Everything I delete reemerges with blue beside (unread). I do not disturb the universe—at least the virtual one—

Spring: smell of thawing dog shit on the walk home from school.

Driving through Troy, which is to say the thought of you, the river still flowing. Where did all the cold go?

Dreamt I wrote my autobiography: the pages were blank, the text in footnotes.

When Aristotle's theory of catharsis—the explanation of which was lost with the second book—and Keats' notion of Negative Capability—a brief mention in a letter—are used as theories, they are projectively filled in by a kind of intellectual Pointillism that creates conceptual bridges across unlinked space the way our perception does between dots in Seurat's paintings.

The very theories are about how we link projectively (through identification, towards resolution), our inability to bear what is before us—the absences, the unknown.

~~The~~ inability to make sense ~~of~~ is how I know it's real—

The redactions are closer to my heart—

From the Q train, which travels above ground over the Manhattan Bridge from Brooklyn to Manhattan, there's a view of the Brooklyn Bridge straddling the East River, the Statue of Liberty, graffiti as familiar now as elderly neighbors on their stoops, laundry lines, Chinatown's tight streets that make me want to reach in and move things around, as in a doll house, carefully, so as to avoid knocking anything over.

I always make sure to position myself before a window, have vowed not to stand with my back to the world, searching my phone. Occasionally, another train passing in the opposite direction, towards Brooklyn, obstructs my view. I've made a game out of trying to catch a glimpse of the carousel near the water in Dumbo, the Staten Island Ferry, or ALPHA MANGO through my window as well as the two windows on either side of the train passing before me, which are constantly swapped out for the windows to their right due to the train's speed—an effect mingling the movement found in 8mm film with nausea. Each time I catch an image through the moving frames of window, I feel a piercing sensation, and think, as Nietzsche did of his aphorisms, *little stabs at happiness—*

I felt a similar piercing as a child, when I used a piece of metal to control light, direct a beam to shine on a specific

point in space, most often the center of my eye—creating
a near-painful but heliodoric effect, as when a character in
a Kieślowski film makes contact with the unknown. This
relationship I imagine being articulated between the universe
and me is parallel to the one I imagine being articulated
inversely, between my unconscious and conscious minds.

As a child, I used to read a series of books about a character
called the Great Brain who was always out-smarting the
neighborhood children. His method of problem solving,
which I've carried with me all these years as precept, was to
enlist his unconscious. He would think of a problem before
going to bed so that the rumination was carried into sleep
and worked through in his dreams. In the history of thought,
there are multiple examples of visionary leaps being made
through dreams. For example, as the story goes, the scientist
that conceived of the benzene molecule being shaped as a ring
saw a vision of snakes biting their own tails. However, even if
it were possible to consciously enlist the unconscious in this
way, in order to do so, you'd have to open yourself up to what
might seep out.

Trusting what comes out of you is not always easy. D.W.
Winnicott described the manifestation of what he termed
the "true self" in the spontaneous gestures of an infant. If
the good-enough mother is able to affirm and accept those
gestures as they are, the "true self" is encouraged to show
itself, whereas the mother who frowns at or corrects the
gestures will condition the infant to replace a spontaneous
gesture with a gesture that will please her—and in this one
sees the birth of the false, socialized self. In the adult world,
those same spontaneous eruptions from our interior (gestures,
sounds, slips of the tongue) incite embarrassment and

repulsion. We board up the access route to the "true self" for reasons having to do with what we believe to be unacceptable (perhaps also to protect what is most precious and vulnerable). But those raw drives are also potential wellsprings for creative spontaneity: "Love the hideous," as Mina Loy has it, "in order to find the sublime core of it."

How, then, does one get at the sublime core? Roland Barthes, in discussing his response to photographs, describes two elements: the studium and the punctum. The studium represents the manifest meaning of a photograph, what is evident to anyone who looks at it, whereas the punctum rises only from certain images that have a chance resonance with one's interior and is experienced as a kind of puncture—an "accident," he writes, "which pricks, bruises me." The punctum is the prick that creates a small pinhole through which something unexpected, unknown, perhaps even alien (with all accompanying hideousness) pokes through.

The series of puncta, the little stabs at happiness, I experience at the window of the Q train make me feel both exhilarated and queasy. Aesthetics, as Freud writes in "The Uncanny," "in general prefer to concern themselves with what is beautiful, attractive and sublime—that is, with feelings of a positive nature—and with the circumstances and the objects that call them forth, rather than with the opposite feelings of repulsion and distress." The punctum, the pinhole through which the unconscious momentarily escapes, can be equally destabilizing as beautiful. "What I can name," writes Barthes, "cannot really prick me."

If what you can name cannot prick you, how can you bring
the punctum into language when interactions with the
world—inner and outer—seem dulled, not pointed enough
to poke through? Such was my dilemma during a period
in which I wasn't able to write anything that felt alive. In
response, I began to use a method of accessing my interior
which involved going to bed with a notebook on my bedside
table, pen marking a blank page, setting my alarm for 3:15
a.m., and, at hearing the alarm, waking for a few seconds to
write down whatever was at the top of my mind—or, perhaps,
as Nietzsche would have it, the bottom ("The 'I' of the lyricist
sounds from the depth of his being: its 'subjectivity' ... is a
fiction"). These Night Fragments, like my little stabs on the Q
train, are pricks made in hopes of releasing brief flashes from
the depth through multiple moving windows:

25.

Why the panic, Alice B. Toklas?
Why the uncooked egg?

10.

It's really only one metaphor in variation.

41.

The moment will be shaken
like a snow globe, a sand globe,
world in eye.

30.

All messy may
All messy maybe.
So messy it can't stay on the page.
A plane flying too low.
An idea like a plane flying
too low.
A person. Like a plane.
Too low flying.
too. loud and louder before
the crash.
It is always Sept 11 in NY.

31.

Sadness folds the chair I would have sat on—

69.

Jeans carry the shape of the person who inhabits them;
if you pick up another person's jeans
you both hold that person and erase them—

16.

Take place out of context & you have time and character.
Being.

20.

At the core of mischief is panic.

16.

The sheet won't stay on the corner of this moment,
keeps pulling up to reveal the blankness beneath.
Elastic gives a false sense of resonance,
like eating grapes.

53.

You think you're going deeper
into the whole,

but are merely skirting the surface
of smaller internal parts—

14.

I lose time trying to figure out
what I already knew,
trying to unsee.

21.

You can see that he's a faintsman—
wild/hunter/warrior—a kind of man
like a kind of bird, wren but not wren.

42.

It has to be put away, the feeling—quick!
drop it into the small pocket, lock it up.

77.

(I was quick to intrude upon the dream to change my outfit)

19.

It's hard to come back
from a grand phase—

morning most difficult,
its shadow a tucked-

under tail bringing us
back to this century.

What century is it?
I can't see your hairstyle.

27.

Part truth is untruth, the way multiplying a negative number with a positive gives you a negative regardless of value.

12.

It's liberating to be cast out—off
everyone's radar—in an open field
without witness—

29.

The end of the earth/
world/conforms only to wind

29.

That is the ugly piece. Taking
the ugly piece so others won't have to.

73.

The dog sleep-shakes a stutter—there's some impediment in
his unconscious tongue.

2.

I hear, Mommy, whispered by the air and jolt up in bed.
Such a plaintive voice, such need—but whose is it, this
suffering?

19.

The black sky absorbs my notion.

52.

Can you know yourself without knowing which direction your gutter leans?

68.

Which era do you think I sing in?

18.

The waves crescendo: the conductor's palms lift great weight skyward.

22.

I smell like the speckles on a lady crab's shell,
land without water. Or land
that has been dipped in water and dried.

78.

Being ▬▬ is dangerous. The faucet is off.

23.

Have I moved out of prototype and into sin?

17.

We do not cook what we
can't understand.
                understand—
the word had to be written twice
to ensure I could read it later.

3.

My mind converting chatter to dissolving pieces of air:
echatteration.

44.

The basis of revolution: we should not be loud in here
(the house, the father's talk of suicide, aftermath).
Is it always mourning for survivors?

&.

Who are you whose story evaporates?
Mourners bend over your body,

the book, murmuring prayers.
I come to pay my respects,

am late to the ceremony,
your story's ascension.
]
]
]
]You will not know in this
lifetime that story, who you are.

Don't fake it (poison).
Muddle through.

42.

I am a character in a landscape
without a story,
the same moment being
repeated again and before—

39.

Sometimes an open field is an empty field,
a lot.
But not much.

17.

What's the gut read?
(I'm shaking dice in my mind in place of thought):
                    snake eyes

38.

It is difficult to get loud
without losing control.

67.

Inside: no thoughts. Just clumping,
clinging to the edge. My thoughts escape
your force field to maintain their integrity.

11.

The night's scratching its head with its hind legs.

97.

Sigmund was small, short-legged and long like a Dachshund.

9.

I needed to check on things,
but I already knew—
so the lesson is to check
on things to see what you know.

58.

Route 6 into Provincetown, Pilgrim Lake
to the right—my heart—

66.

I'm sure I'm breaking the rules—
let me hear them from the ones who care.

9.

Why do scabs itch? Wasn't the initial pain enough?

On the local platform at 86th Street waiting for a 6 Train, I noticed, written on a column in thick Sharpie, "Fuck Lyric:"

FUCK LYRIC

I felt stunned, stood staring so long at those two words I almost missed the train that briefly opened its light to me. Of course, I thought later, it's possible there's some asshole named Lyric somewhere in New York City who needs to fuck off. But the message, as I took it, resonates with a struggle I've had for years with poetics, the figure of address, and larger questions of selfhood.

It all began in a barn in Provincetown. I was grappling with the recognition that even though I'd developed an aversion to confessional poetry, the poems I found moving, which served as my measure of a poem's value, were invariably lyric, written in the first person and addressed—as is all speech—to a second person, whether circumscribed or implied, a *you* without whom the poem wouldn't, or, perhaps couldn't, have been written. There I was, off-season, at land's edge, in a world populated by Portuguese fishermen and an erasing darkness that set in by mid-afternoon. There I was, but where were *you*?

I am never merely writing, but always writing *to you*. In response to a college friend's praise of her letters, Marianne Moore responded, "My letters are better than my stories I suppose because I am not self-conscious. Because I am thinking of '*you*' (~~whoever you are~~)." The *you* of any letter is inevitably multiple, at once the letter's explicit addressee, an unknown *you* "(whoever you are)," but also the unknown you struck-out "(~~whoever you are~~)," which may be a shift back to a known you or another shift away. *You* become a position that figures pass through, momentarily occupy:

Marcet

you

whoever you are

(~~whoever you are~~)

But if *you* are an endless chain of metonymic displacements, then what am *I*, that self that organizes around thinking of *you?* And why is it that writing a lyric poem that has an *I* that matches up with the person I consider myself to be in my everyday life induces shame? How can the *I* of a poem— also a chain of metonymic displacements—maintain the same multiplicity as *you*, resist adopting a fiction of a singular voice, have the intimate quality of a notebook without the intimate content, become the position or mouthpiece through which the world, rather than an individual, speaks?

The writer who has at no point belonged anywhere, who like Edmond Jabès' Yukel, has never been at ease in his own skin, lives life in the "elsewhere," a province of exile, a region reached through the movement of the pen that collapses winter with autumn, summer with spring, past with future, night with day—but also the embodied self with concurrent selves in alternate space-times. The one who speaks "I" becomes a

Yukel, you have never been at ease in your own skin. You have never been here, but always elsewhere, ahead of yourself or behind like winter in the eyes of autumn or summer in the eyes of spring, in the past or in the future like those syllables whose passage from night to day is so much like lightning that it merges with the movement of the pen.

many who speaks "I" or "he" while meaning "I" and "he," but also "you," "we" and "they." My attempt to make sense of this voice that speaks as one but out of the many—first, second and third person simultaneously—led nowhere, into the nowhere of the mind, which is also an elsewhere, and, like the unconscious, a space of possibility.

And so it arrived that way, as a fragment in the voice of dream, "The fourth person singular exists in the fourth dimension." Yet how does one decipher here into logic what was already known, but only elsewhere—ahead, behind and out of skin?

"There are things we've never seen, heard or even felt," wrote Kafka in a letter, "and we can't prove they exist, though no one has yet tried, but we run after them, without knowing which direction to run in, and we catch up with them without reaching them, and, still complete with clothes, family souvenirs and social relationships, we fall into them as into a grave that was only a shadow on the road." The runners Kafka refers to in this passage—running after "things" they have "never seen, heard or even felt," things they "can't prove ... exist"—make up a "we," but also a "no one," having not "yet tried" to prove the existence of the perceived "things." This trial exists in the future, a future containing the things we will run after but "catch up with ... without reaching"—the Real we search for but never find—because we live in the shadow of things, even a grave, fall even into the shadow of our own death, which is the point of certainty toward which every being is supposedly running. A runner of the we, who is also no one, exits the world of proof and enters a shadow region, a region whose fourth dimension has an elsewhere that relegates us to a space-time in which we will always "catch up ... without reaching."

Four-dimensional space-time takes into account three dimensions of space and a fourth dimension of time. A point (P) existing at a particular location in space at a particular time is called an "event." Before Einstein's theory of special relativity, time and space were thought to be absolute: absolute time was thought to exist independently of space, absolute space thought to have a physical reality independent of any object. Einstein demonstrated that objects, rather than existing in space, are spatially extended, which makes the concept of "empty space" impossible. If you transpose his theory to time, "now" also loses its meaning as an absolute because a specific event exists only in the context of a specific frame of reference. If a self were thought of within this context of four dimensions, there would also be no absolute self or identity (I). Similarly spatially extended, (I) would exist within but also beyond, out of, skin.

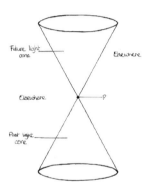

In the diagram above, originally presented by Stephen Hawking, a specific event is termed (P). All events that can be affected by what happens at (P) by particles or waves traveling at or below the speed of light are in or on the future light cone of (P), while all events that can affect (P) by a particle or wave traveling at or below the speed of light are in the past light cone of (P). All other events are in the elsewhere of (P), where they have no effect on and are not affected by what happens at (P). If the sun ceased to shine, Hawking proposes, because the sun is in our elsewhere and light takes eight minutes to travel from the sun into our future light cone, events on earth would be affected only after an eight-minute lag.

This lag, in relation to an individual, would perhaps represent happenings in the elsewhere of our psychic structure that we do not feel the effects of simultaneous to their occurrence, similar to what, in psychoanalytic temporality, is described by Freud as *Nachträglichkeit*, translated by Lacan as *après-coup* and later put into English by Jean Laplanche as *afterwardness*. *Nachträglichkeit* describes another kind of lag, in which what is experienced by a person in the present has already happened in the past, but in a form that they weren't able to assimilate into meaning and therefore, rather than registering consciously, left unconscious psychical traces.

Winnicott describes a similar dynamic in which a person fears finding a "detail" from the past that is, ironically, "compulsively looked for in the future." The lag here is in the registration of an event in consciousness rather than in space-time.

This compulsive search in the future for something from the past can take the form of writing. Gerard Manley Hopkins: "my lament/ Is cries countless, cries like dead letters sent/ To dearest him that lives alas! away."

When the unconscious, which remains for the most part in the elsewhere, makes its way into our past light cone—affecting (P) and (I) in the present—or makes its way into our future light cone—affecting (P) and (I) in the future—it becomes conscious, but in a form that is altered due to a variation in vantage point. We are always operating with this lag to a degree, even neurologically, as what we experience as *now* is, in fact, about eight milliseconds in the past, as that is the time it takes the brain to process and put together data into a conscious representation. There is, in other words, no present—and time isn't linear. The past and the future do not merely affect the present, but represent themselves as separate subjects that cannot be easily assimilated into our understanding of a particular moment.

When the woman from the past asks the protagonist of Chris Marker's *La Jetée* about his necklace— "the combat necklace he wore at the start of the war that is to break out some day"— he "invents an explanation."

Being moved to write lyric poetry is a kind of compulsion to invent explanations as a way of searching for and attempting to master what you fear finding that has already been experienced, an unthought known or a known that has been thought by a version of self that is yet to come, that is confined to catching up without reaching.

By the time our perception of ourselves registers, we have already moved on (however slightly) from that particular self and are looking back from a distance (however miniscule), so that the perceived *I* has become a *not-I*. This outside perspective on oneself can provide a basis for shame, which involves looking back at the self through the eyes of another. It also makes of the surrounding selves, in the past and future light cones, neighbor selves, who should indeed be loved, but as *whom?* (Lacan points out that most people hate themselves.)

Years ago, reading André Breton's *Mad Love*, I was struck by the line, "One must always live as if on the brink of love!" I carried it around as precept, but when I turned back to the book to refind the sentence, it wasn't there. I'm certain Breton wrote it, but, at this point (P), Breton and the past self that was moved by Breton are equally separate subjects that have traveled out of my past light cone and into my Elsewhere—

We superimpose ourselves onto others each time we address them, which is another way our neighbors become other kinds of self. When we construct any form of speech that we plan to address to another, there's a split second in which we exit our own position and imaginatively project ourselves into the position of the other person to envision their response to what we plan to say, and then quickly edit our speech to accommodate that imagined reception. Bakhtin calls this dynamic *addressivity*: our dialogue is, at first, always internal, a communication between the self and a psychic representation of another person. We do a sort of test drive in our minds on our imagined representation of the other before taking our speech into the world and addressing it to the living, thinking, feeling person before us.

The irony here is that it is our own mind projectively externalized that makes us cower, a mind we imaginatively create for the other that can never match up with the contents of their actual mind. Lyric address, then, occurs not only between an I and a you, but between separate parts of mind and different states of self. We use our expectations of how people (or versions of ourselves) we've known well have responded in the past as an index when anticipating how the person before us will respond in the present. Freud called this dynamic transference—we transfer our expectations and feelings about known figures onto someone in the moment in order to figure them out— which is, in a sense, *Nachträglichkeit* inverted, the past resignifying the future as opposed to the past being given meaning retroactively. He

> What is your aim in philosophy?— To show the fly the way out of the fly-bottle.

believed that analyzing the transference was the key to a psychoanalytic cure: it helps people develop the ability to be conscious of what is happening in the moment, as well as what had traveled from the elsewhere to affect it, so that they have the opportunity to make choices about how to behave in the present rather than acting on a kind of autopilot.

> "Beyond being, is a Third person who is not defined by selfhood."

Psychoanalysis is, therefore, also lyric, involves an I addressing a thou, a patient addressing an analyst, a present self addressing a past self, a past self addressing a present self, an address from an imagined mind (as with addressivity) or a message transmitted to or from a Third, now

> Who is the third who walks always beside you?
> When I count, there are only you and I together
> But when I look ahead up the white road
> There is always another one walking beside you
> Gliding wrapt in a brown mantle, hooded
> I do not know whether a man or a woman
> —But who is that on the other side of you?

in our elsewhere, which will only register later, afterwards, if we can catch up and reach it.

Four-dimensional space-time is always relational, and to speak about the absolute past and absolute future in light cones is to have always already chosen a fixed observer. Moore lived with her mother until she died. Her mother was, in many ways, an inhibiting force Moore had to get away from early in her career in order to write. Moore, yearning to be part of a literary community, wrote, early in her career, poems addressed to literary figures she admired—"To Bernard Shaw: A Prize Bird," "To Browning." Those early lyric poems are filled with emotion—in fact, "To Browning" is based on love letters between Robert Browning and Elizabeth Barrett Browning in which they discuss a yellow rose, infidelity, their passion. In Moore's poem, she steps into their circuit of communication—not quite as Browning, but to the side of him, to enter their discussion and then to address a version of Browning himself. These early poems, essentially odes, are (for her) quite charged.

When her first book, *Selected Poems*, was published, however, she replaced each title that had addressed a poem to a specific figure with an impersonal title—"To Robert Browning" became "Injudicious Gardening," for example—and addressed the

Dedications imply giving, and we do not care to make a gift of what is insufficient; but in my immediate family there is one "who thinks in a particular way;" and I should like to add that where there is an effect of thought or pith in these pages, the thinking and often the actual phrases are hers.

entire collection to her mother in a postscript at the end of the book. In redressing the address, particularly in addressing the poems to an inhibiting figure, the emotion in the poems—even as the poems were essentially the same beyond their titles—escaped.

A circuit of communication plays into the construction of any utterance and involves our past selves, figures from our past that communicate unconsciously with us and have shaped our expectations, the person before us whose reception of our speech we anticipate and restructure around, the voices and objects in our external and internal worlds. Any utterance is a record of the four-dimensional space-time surrounding a moment—the (I), the past and future light cones, everything in the elsewhere and the lag created as something in the elsewhere moves towards our future or out of our past light cones—a period during which we experience psychical traces of things we may perceive but cannot know. Perhaps Moore was "not self-conscious" when "thinking of *you* (~~whoever you are~~)" because her addressee occupied a position that Bakhtin terms a *superaddressee*, a "(third), whose absolutely just understanding is presumed," or what Michael Warner calls an "indefinite strange[r]," a figure that allows you to speak into a "social imaginary," an "environment of strangerhood [that] is the necessary premise of some of our most prized ways of being." Only to this *you* can one speak as (I), in the fourth person singular. You are that indefinite stranger. Can you hear me? I'm writing from elsewhere. This book is for *you* (~~whoever you are~~).

My dear, accept this dedication; it is given over, as it were, blindfolded, but therefore undisturbed by any consideration, in sincerity. Who you are, I know not; where you are, I know not; what your name is, I know not. Yet you are my hope, my pride, and my unknown honor.

Sketch 37

On the way home from a walk, my dog likes to return to spots
he has pissed on to smell (& sometimes lick) his markings.
Such joy goes into this sniffing, while Slavoj Žižek describes
the revulsion most of us feel in perceiving our interiors erupt
into the external world through the example of saliva, which
we constantly produce and swallow inside our bodies. Imagine,
he proposes, a scenario in which someone tells you to spit into
a glass, then drink it. The thought is repulsive: your insides
are to remain hidden, even from yourself. The lyric is that

kuntaton: most   saliva in a glass, but what does it incarnate?
doglike, most
shameless—

Sketch 53

Wilson's Plover, distraction displays—
feigning weakness to draw predatory attention
to a different stretch of beach, far from nest.
Self as beach—expanse of stable ground
emerging from ocean (the unconscious).
Did I plover last night (broken wing, mock
brooding) to guard against envy? A kind
of psychic autocorrect: *Let's go solve where else.*

Sketch 1

Pagina after pagina in Marlene Dumas' book.
Is it page in Dutch? Vagina in midnight blue?
Self-portrait of womb: 'DARK BLACK LONELY
SPACE', Louise Bourgeois, 'Deep inside my heart'—
or is it Tracey Emin?—(2009-2010), the empty years.
What will be born of this splotch of blue, sea horse
on wheels? How much beeldenstorm swims inside me?

Sketch 27

A man entered the subway car at Borough Hall,
was about to sit, but just as his knees began to bend
the train jerked into motion. He stood up, as though
regaining composure after a brief humiliation,
as though it were somehow shameful to be subject
to gravity's impersonal force, caught
in its grip, an object controlled by physics.

Sketch 19

A woman in high heels walks slowly along the broken avenue.
The boys tangle their leashes trying to get ahead, turn and
look back at her, then veer up the hill towards the open
field. The park can't contain their desire. It pours into the
atmosphere in particles that speed and collide, cause small
children to lose their balance and fall off their bikes. This is
quantum entanglement on an unseasonably warm November
afternoon, the smell of coffee from Bittersweet that makes me
bend backwards into morning, the spring of another year, trip
while rushing home to meet you—

I send them into another room so I can think. They fill me with their *gift given—stolen—want it back—never! too precious* refuse. I block out the chatter until one calls, *How do you spell anguish?* I spell and feel it at the same time, think, if I had a stutter I'd trip on the *gui*—it is in pain but also in guise, as my pain is in my guise, the many roles I play on autopilot.

From the northwest:
a crow, a caw,
a flapparition.

Look! calls my daughter, *Two monarchs!* The butterflies flap, milkweed to daisies and asters, blazing star. She reminds me they are poisonous. *Is everything beautiful poisonous?* I ask. *It's the milkweed that's poisonous*, she explains. *Not to them, but to you.*

Today was the kind of day in which only two heels of bread remained. As a child, I referred to them as the ugly pieces. Now, I disguise them by flipping the outside inward when making a sandwich for my daughters. Why can't I let them be ugly?

Low tide. I park the car, get out, pick a blade of dune grass and slip it into my notebook. What is my song of self? I hear nothing but waves and crow.

River of want: dare I dip my children in these waters?

I wish for the dew to burn off, but wish it with aggression. Some part of me feels nihilistic, like spitting out.

Braiding my hair, she says, *Now you're going to be the prettiest girl at work.* Then, pointing to *The Purloined Poe*, she tells me, *Take that book with you.* —Why? —*Because people are going to think you're nasty.* —How will the book change that? —*Just take it! It's a secret... don't tell anyone.*

A crow caws in twos—four, six, then the old oddity slipping in. If I figure out the direction of the calls will I understand my desire?

I lost much of yesterday to sadness, panic of not knowing—& later to the dream in which I drove despite the sticky windshield, sleeping children—maternal dread—

At night, she cried, despairing: *I just realized, for the rest of my life, I'll keep getting older. I'll never grow backwards and be a baby again.*

At dawn, an orange bird stands out against the grey morning. The knowns have made their migration. It's time to follow an unidentifiable wing.

She stands before the digital clock, waiting for the ones' spot to change from 9 to 0. *I have to see this.* As she waits silently, I, too, return to zero. Freud talks about pleasure as a state of minimal stimulation, *nirvana*. I am permitted this pleasure by proxy, like the alcoholic Anna Freud describes who stopped drinking but woke each night to put water out for the cat. The thirst was there, but displaced onto the cat to be satisfied.

butcher boy
Maisie

I don't want to knock the world that way, destructively.

Other people can't hear your thoughts, right? She asks, looking about the train, suspiciously.

Prime number: piece of hard candy that never dissolves. We are three, my daughters and I: the three of me.

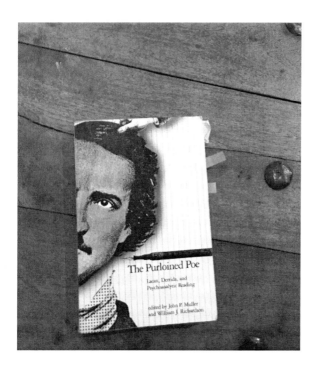

Sketch 64

Pleasure and disgust, the border of desire, of aesthetics,
where beauty and the uncanny meet—is this the brink
one must always live on, bare and bear, the vulnerability
necessitated in feeling alive? When I have bared myself, I
feel a compulsion to send out a flurry of signals to adjust the
reception of others, to scramble the image that may have been
momentarily revealed of me—

Sketch 7

If only you knew what I saw when I looked at your face, headless motherfucker, with your head turned around. We do that kind of shit. We know everything. That's how we train. We know fucking everything.

As I switched subway cars at the next stop, I saw others who had stood beside him rush to do the same. It's that easy to unknow, to deny that we are at war.

Sketch 4

How did the caterpillar feel when it crawled out of its face,
left it behind in mulch at the bottom of its jar? Is this
ahistoricity, to go forth having molted your face and all
associations dragged along?

Sketch 13

The wet in the air is like signal anxiety: life is about to change. The parked bicycle's front wheel indicates the direction gravity has chosen, the ice cream truck emits music & fumes outside the school, luring children, as did the Pied Piper, towards death. Robert Browning wrote a poem about the Pied Piper of Hamelin, a rat catcher who passed through Germany in the middle ages, which was published in *Dramatic Lyrics* in 1842. After being trashed for his confessional lyrics in his first book, *Pauline: A Fragment of A Confession*, which didn't sell a single copy, Browning veered sharply away from confessional poetry and invented the dramatic monologue, which, using historical figures as mouthpieces, protected him from lyric shame. Once, when I was part of a dance troupe, we rehearsed our upcoming show wearing masks. Never before had I felt so free—sometimes you can put more of your emotion into art by keeping your face out. Or is thinking that way merely projective autobiography?

"[S]elf," wrote Shelley in a letter, "that burr that sticks to one. I can't seem to get it off."

∀utobiography

⊆

∅

ɤ

꒓

⊆   I wonder if the person who found my notebook is now having thoughts that I've repressed.

∅   Childhood: loved & unknown.

ɤ   As I lay in bed reading *My Struggle*, a mosquito flew towards the page. I tried to close the book on it, but it darted away too quickly. I stayed up much of the night hoping to refind my prey, but no-see-um. That is my struggle, unseeing—or, rather, seeing then (no-see-) um-seeing—

꒓ Can't eat, can't sleep—I'm burning in the St. Augustine way (*To Clinton Hill then I came, burning, burning*—)

~

∀

∠

꒓

~ A little bit wild, close to the core, hyperlive—

∀ I have just returned from a party of which I was the life
and soul; wit poured from my lips, everyone laughed and
admired me—but I went away—and the dash should be as
long as the earth's orbit--
--and wanted
to shoot myself.

∠ The phone rang, but there was no one on the other end.
It threw me, untethered, out of orbit. I cried while washing
dishes, my head full of yellow light like the Saver's Discount
awning.

꒓ On the elevator wall:

       o
  N O P∧E T S

Π

ς

τ

~

φ

Π The spider in my ear: my daughter's fear of what's inside of me is really a fear of what's inside of her (all of us) & may crawl out at any second—

ς I can taste the mollusk, but can't find the room.

τ   LOST TIME
              (EROS)

~ Nothing seems to matter, have weight—up with the baby at night, sleepwalking the day; a spoon floats at the same level as *Ecce Homo*, a bottle of Wite-Out—no gravity, meaning, gravitas—

φ The realization that I'm invisible to the people I'm close to and visible only to those one step away.

}

|

χ

¬

}   Self-congratulation: bucket of mop water dumped into the sound of applause.

| There will be no revelation—only seaweed in your bathing suit, awareness of the endless not-me that can be pulled off your naked skin and tossed away.

χ   syncope

¬   New Year's Eve: there are four minutes left in the delivery window. I wait for a new oven that has been about to arrive for six hours.

⌐

⇒

)

≈

⌐ ▬▬▬▬▬▬▬▬▬▬▬▬▬▬▬▬▬ Is there
more you want to tell me?—▬▬▬▬▬▬▬▬▬▬▬▬▬
▬▬▬▬▬▬▬▬▬▬▬▬▬▬▬▬▬▬ A precise
missile, as ▬▬▬ put it. To be doubly abandoned.

⇒   Ah, the disruption of my phantasy! The lie the world
gives rudely, repeatedly—

)   Panic is a frayed tether. What does it tie me to?

≈   If I have almonds, I will eat almonds. But if I don't
have almonds, will I think of them? Do we think of what
we don't have, or is thinking a kind of having—having
a kind of thinking, as with the characters in *Gulliver's
Travels* who carry the objects they need in conversation in
sacks on their backs. If you want to let go of something,
you have to let go of the thought of it. Last night I dreamt
a text message, "Darling..." then a line of code. Numbers
and letters, but the meaning? Or is the message empty,
the code impossible to crack, its only communication, *keep
thinking, holding on?*

Γ

/

∞

∪

σ

Γ If you work too hard on anything it turns to shit,
children sculpting with Play-Doh, not knowing when to
walk away, all colors to brown.

/ A woman seated on the edge of a subway bench placed
her index finger against the wall as if to balance herself
as the subway careened into a sharp turn. I feel that way
today—I'm using a mere digit to try and exert some control
over a situation that leaves me powerless, unknowing, an
unmoored particle in space—

∞ *Then how do you account for your being child-like?* He
asked. *Have you thought about that?*

∪ The gyroscopic function of unconscious fantasy: the
main thing it balances is shame. That's what really throws us
off.

σ The moral is, of course, don't write one-act plays.

Move towards what you believe in and the person you are
steps through—

ᴐ   [punctuation of grief]

Notes

I have corrected here any passages that I have misremembered and used in misremembered form within the book.

"From a certain point on, there is no more turning back. That is the point that must be reached." Franz Kafka, *The Zurau Aphorisms*, trans. Roberto Calasso, New York: Shocken Books 2006, p. 7.

"Transparence interests me. I want to be transparent. If people could see through me, they could not help loving me, forgive me." Louise Bourgeois, *Grand Street* 65 (1998), p. 38.

"Why do you talk so much? What is it that you have to hide?" La Rochefoucauld quoted in Louise Bourgeois, *Return of the Repressed*, vol 2, Violette Editions: London 2012, p. 11.

"I know, I feel/ the meaning that words hide;/ they are anagrams, cryptograms/ little boxes, conditioned/ to hatch butterflies... " H.D, *Trilogy*, New York: New Directions 1973, p. 53.

"Don't waste your energy and your time—which belong to God—throwing stones at the dogs that bark at you on the way. Ignore them." Josemaría Escrivá, *The Way*, New York: Scepter Publishers 1992, p. 23.

"Man's flight from mystery towards what is readily available, onward from one current thing to the next, passing the mystery by—this is erring." Martin Heidegger, "On the Essence of Truth," in *Basic Writings*, D.F. Krell (ed.), London: Routledge 1978, p. 133.

"I want to be/ at least as alive as the vulgar." Frank O'Hara, "My Heart" in *The Selected Poems of Frank O'Hara*, Donald Allen (ed.), New York: Vintage Books 1974, p. 99.

"God will vomit out the lukewarm." Josemaría Escrivá, *The Way*, New York: Image/ Doubleday 2006, p. 55.

"A man possesses himself in flashes, and even when he does possess himself he does not quite overtake himself." Antonin Artaud, *Artaud Anthology*, Jack Hirschman (ed.), San Francisco: City Lights Books 1963, p. 20.

"The Other Person is always perceived as an other, but in its concept it is the condition for all perception, for others as for ourselves. It is the condition for our passing from one world to another." Gilles Deleuze and Felix Guattari, *What Is Philosophy*, trans. Graham Burchell and Hugh Tomlinson, New York: Columbia University Press 1996, pp. 18-19.

"I don't sleep. My neighbor has a dog and whenever it starts barking I run to the window. I don't want them to cut me up like a chicken." Translated from an interview with a man in a war zone on National Public Radio's *All Things Considered*.

"Love the hideous, in order to find the sublime core of it." Mina Loy, "Aphorisms on Futurism" in Rogor Conover (ed.) *The Lost Lunar Baedeker: Poems of Mina Loy*, New York: Farrar, Strauss and Giroux 1996, p. 149.

"A photograph's *punctum* is that accident which pricks me (but also bruises me, is poignant to me)." Roland Barthes, *Camera Lucida*, trans. Richard Howard, New York: Hill and Wang 1980, p. 27.

"Aesthetics in general prefer to concern themselves with what is beautiful, attractive and sublime—that is, with feelings of a positive nature—and with the circumstances and the objects that call them forth, rather than with the opposite feelings of repulsion and distress." Sigmund Freud, "The 'Uncanny'" in *The Standard Edition of the Complete Psychological Works of Sigmund Freud*, vol *XVII* (1917-1919), trans. J. Strachey, London: The Hogarth Press and The Institute of Psychoanalysis 1953-73, p. 217-256.

"What I can name cannot really prick me." Barthes, p. 51.

"The 'I' of the lyricist sounds from the depth of his being: its 'subjectivity' … is a fiction." Friedrich Nietzsche, The Birth of Tragedy, trans. Walter Kaufmann, New York: Vintage Books, 1967, p. 49.

"My letters are better than my stories I suppose because I am not self-conscious. Because I am thinking of 'you' (~~whoever you are~~)." Marianne Moore, The Selected Letters of Marianne Moore, New York: Alfred A. Knopf 1997, pp. 40-41.

"Yukel, you have never been at ease in your own skin. You have never been here, but always elsewhere, ahead of yourself or behind like winter in the eyes of autumn or summer in the eyes of spring, in the past or in the future like those syllables whose passage from night to day is so much like lightening that it merges with the movement of the pen." Edmond Jabès, The Book of Questions, trans. Rosmarie Waldrop, Middletown: Wesleyan University Press 1991, p. 32.

"There are things we have never seen, heard, or even felt, whose existence moreover cannot be proved—although no one has yet tried to prove them—which we nevertheless run in pursuit of, even though the direction of their course has never been seen, and which we catch up with before we have reached them, and into which we someday fall with clothes, family mementos, and social relationships as into a pit that was only a shadow on the road." Letter to Max Brod 15 December 1908. Franz Kafka, Letters to Friends, Family and Editors, New York: Knopf Doubleday Publishing Group 2013, pp. 47-48.

Explanations, examples, and the diagram of four dimensional space-time come from Chapter 2 of Stephen Hawking, A Brief History of Time, New York: Bantam Books 1998, pp. 24-36.

D.W. Winnicott "Fear of Breakdown," in The International Review of Psychoanalysis, vol 1 1974, pp. 103-7.

"[M]y lament/ Is cries countless, cries like dead letters sent/ To dearest him that lives alas! away." Gerard Manley Hopkins, "I Wake And Feel the Fell of Dark Not Day" in *The Poems of Gerard Manley Hopkins*, London: Oxford University Press 1967, p. 101.

"What we experience as now is, in fact, about eight milliseconds in the past because that is the time it takes the brain to process data and put it together into a conscious representation," Sean Carroll, "Why Does Time Exist," http://www.npr.org/programs/ted-radio-hour/?showDate=2016-08-05.

La Jetée, Chris Marker. Argos films, 1963.

The concept of addressivity, M. M. Bakhtin, *Problems of Dostoevsky's Poetics*, trans. Carly Emerson, Minneapolis: University of Minnesota Press 1984, p. 95.

"What is your aim in philosophy?—To show the fly the way out of the fly-bottle." Ludwig Wittgenstein, *Philosophical Investigations*, trans. G.E.M. Anscombe, 3rd ed., Oxford: Blackwell 1995, 1:309.

"Beyond being is a Third person who is not defined by selfhood." Emmanuel Levinas, quoted in Maurice Blanchot, *The Writing of the Disaster*, Lincoln: New Bison Books 1995, pp. 23-4.

"Who is the third who walks always beside you?/ When I count, there are only you and I together/ But when I look ahead up the white road/ There is always another one walking beside you/ Gliding wrapt in a brown mantle, hooded/ I do not know whether a man or a woman/ —But who is that on the other side of you?" T.S. Eliot, *The Waste Land and Other Poems*, Boston: Houghton Mifflin Harcout 1962, p. 43.

"Dedications imply giving, and we do not care to make a gift of what is insufficient; but in my immediate family there is one 'who thinks in a particular way;' and I should like to add that where there is an effect of thought or pith in these pages, the thinking and often the actual phrases are hers." Marianne Moore, *Selected Poems*, New York: Macmillan Co. 1935, p. 108.

The concept of the "supersaddresee," M.M. Bakhtin, *Problems of Dostoevsky's Poetics*, trans. Carly Emerson, Minneapolis: University of Minnesota Press 1984, p. 126.

The concept of an "indefinite stranger" as a figure that allows you to speak into a "social imaginary," an "environment of strangerhood [that] is the necessary premise of some of our most prized ways of being." Michael Warner, *Publics and Counterpublics*, New York: Zone Books 2002, pp. 74-75.

"My dear, accept this dedication; it is given over, as it were, blindfolded, but therefore undisturbed by any consideration, in sincerity. Who you are, I know not; where you are, I know not; what your name is, I know not. Yet you are my hope, my pride, and my unknown honor." Søren Kierkegaard, *The Crowd is Untruth*, trans. Charles K. Bellinger, New York: Merchant Books 2014, p. 1.

"Far-seeing Sybil, forever hidden,/ come out of your cave at last/ And speak to us in the poet's voice/ the voice of the fourth person singular/ the voice of the inscrutable future/ the voice of the people mixed/ with a wild soft laughter—/ And give us new dreams to dream,/ Give us new myths to live by!" Lawrence Ferlinghetti, "To The Oracle At Delphi," *San Francisco Poems*, San Francisco: City Lights Foundation 2001, p. 80-81. Gilles Deleuze picks up on Ferlinghetti's "fourth person singular" as he describes what happens when "the dissolved self, the cracked I, the lost identity...cease to be buried and begin...to liberate the singularities of the surface" (*The Logic of Sense*, trans. Mark Lester, New York: Columbia University Press 1990, p. 141).

"Take a glass, spit in it...look and then try to drink it. You cannot, because it's outside. It's disgusting, it's disgusting." Slavoj Žižek, https://biblioklept.org/2011/04/11/ david-foster-wallace-slavoj-zizek-and-toilet-ideology/

"*[S]elf*, that burr that will stick to one. I can't get it off yet."
Percy Bysshe Shelley, *The Selected Letters of Percy Bysshe Shelley*,
vol 1, F.L. Jones (ed.), Oxford: Clarendon Press 1964, p. 109.

"I have just returned from a party of which I was the life and
soul; wit poured from my lips, everyone laughed and admired
me—but I went away—and the dash should be as long as the
earth's orbit--
--and wanted to shoot myself."
Søren Kirkegaard, *The Journals of Søren Kirkegaard*, Alexander
Dru (ed.), London: Oxford University Press 1938, p. 27.

Acknowledgments

Grateful acknowledgment is made to the editors and curators of the following publications and organizations in and at which portions of this book first appeared: *The Awl*, *Granta*, *Poetry London*, *Provincetown Arts*, *tender*, The Freud Museum in London, The Poetry Society in London, The Scottish Poetry Library, The Sutton Gallery and The University of Liverpool.

Thank you also to The Fine Arts Work Center in Provincetown and the Norman Mailer Center.

To the entire team that worked on this book, particularly Alison Welsby, Natalie Bolderston, Rachel Clarke, and the brilliant Deryn Rees-Jones, thank you.

Thank you to Sarah Goh for her drawing of four-dimensional spacetime on page 41.

Enormous gratitude to my parents, to Josh Cohen, Rich Cohen, Sophie Collins, Rosie Dastgir, Jeff Dolven, Nick Flynn, Liz Hildreth, Ellen Gallagher, Ben Kafka, Chris Knutsen, Lily Koppel, Elizabeth Rubin, Sarah Schulman, Gilda Sherwin, and, especially, Kathryn Maris.

And, finally, gratitude and awe to Isadora and Sabine for their drawings on pages 5 and 47, respectively, and for transmitting additional voices into my mind—